SAN FRANCISCO

SAN FRA

PHOTOGRAPHS BY

FOREWORD BY

NCISCO

SANTI VISALLI

KEVIN STARR

UNIVERSE

Page 1: Fisherman's Wharf

Pages 2–3: Windsurfing on the bay against the backdrop of Alcatraz Island

Page 5: Multicolored souvenirs await their new owners on Pier 39

Published in the United States of America in 1995 by
UNIVERSE PUBLISHING
A Division of Rizzoli International Publications, Inc.
300 Park Avenue South, New York, NY 10010

Clothbound edition first published in the United States of America in 1990 by
Rizzoli International Publications, Inc.

95 96 97 98 99 / 10 9 8 7 6 5 4 3 2 1

Library of Congress catalog card number: 95-060819

Design by Gilda Hannah

Printed in Korea

Dedicated to my wife Gayla, a native San Franciscan

FOREWORD

KEVIN STARR

In San Francisco, Europe and the Americas have joined Asia and the Pacific Basin to create a jewel city of enchantment. San Francisco has been called Everyone's Favorite City. No wonder: the world, with its diversity of peoples and cultures, has participated in the making of this urban masterpiece. Visitors behold something that is their own in San Francisco, and they in turn are grateful for this subtle compliment of cultural reinforcement. From this perspective, San Francisco possesses world-city status despite its small size and population.

The City of Saint Francis embodies an ideal, a hope that the peoples of the planet might live peaceably together, in a city built to celebrate beauty and the good life. The ancient Phoenician city of Byblos was such a city, intimate, polyglot, soaked in memory; and so too was the eclectic Hellenic colony of Alexandria in Egypt. History raises certain smaller port cities above the regional, San Francisco among them, endowing them with a special responsibility for beauty and remembrance, as well as for trade and finance. Like Byblos and Alexandria, San Francisco is charged with a cultural mission of being a port city intensely expressive of urban culture and cosmopolitan value. If the United States had no San Francisco, it would have to remedy the deficiency; every civilization needs a crossroads city, preferably on the sea, to embody the best possibilities of civic culture.

Santi Visalli presents us with elegant images, grand and intimate alike, of the special instance of history and civility called San Francisco. Born and educated in Italy, Santi Visalli has been practicing photography in the United States since 1959. How appropriate that this preeminent Euro-American should choose to interpret a city which most visitors find so European in ambiance. The descendent of a race of citybuilders, Santi Visalli perceives and captures on film that which is elemental and archetypal. He concerns himself with elemental urban forms—bridges, skyscrapers, hotels, parks, museums, sacred places—which he presents with an emphasis upon their universality.

As an achieved urban environment, San Francisco participates in the universal forms and functions of great cities around the globe. In this book, Santi Visalli explores a paradigm of urban form; San Francisco, the smallest possible world city in its physical dimensions, offers the distilled essence of all urban structures and experience. There is no aspect of the world city that is not represented in San Francisco in one way or another. This completeness, this capacity to encompass on a compact scale the range and diversity of urbanism, plays a major part in conferring upon the City of Saint Francis its universal acceptance as an urban archetype. A remarkable confluence of geography, history, and a photogenic built environment at the northern front of a mountainous peninsula running between San Francisco Bay and the Pacific Ocean, has given each element of the urban prototype for the Ferry Building, which opened in July 1898.) In 1905 Daniel Hudson Burnham, apostle extraordinary of the City Beautiful movement, completed a comprehensive plan for San Francisco. After the earthquake and fire, the Burnham Plan inspired the reconstruction of the Civic Center along City Beautiful lines. Another Beaux Arts graduate, Arthur Brown, Jr., designed the City Hall in 1913 as the focal point for what many critics believe is the finest civic center complex in the nation. The oxidized copper dome of City Hall is fourteen feet higher than that of the nation's capitol and looms above an ensemble of Beaux Arts buildings: Arthur Brown's War Memorial Opera House; Skidmore, Owings & Merrill's Louise M. Davies Symphony Hall; and the Edmund G. Brown State Office Building at McAllister and Van Ness, the most recent addition to the Civic Center.

The post–1906 earthquake generation built grandly because it envisioned San Francisco as a world city introducing European civilization to the Pacific Rim, and Asian culture to the United States and Europe. A city with such an important mission required public buildings evocative of the capital cities of Europe. And besides, did not San Francisco call itself the Paris of the West? The City of Paris rotunda, designed in 1909 by Willis Polk, skillfully reinstated into the Neiman Marcus building on Union Square in the mid-1980s, asserts this Parisian identification, as does the California Palace of the Legion of Honor at Lincoln Park, donated to San Francisco by Adolph and Alma de Bretteville Spreckels in 1924 as a memorial to the American dead of World War I.

Like many other American cities, San Francisco is in the process of reevaluating the architectural era that followed the American Renaissance and Beaux Arts Revival, which is to say, the Gothic, Art Deco, and Moderne eras of the 1920s and 1930s. A study of the

period's skyscrapers must include the Russ Building on Montgomery Street, which for so many years was the signature building on the San Francisco skyline, along with Timothy Pflueger's Pacific Bell Building on New Montgomery. Most conspicuous of the Moderne monuments is Coit Tower atop Telegraph Hill. Financed by a bequest from Lillie Hitchcock Coit, a native daughter who spent most of her life in France, Coit Tower was designed in 1933 by Arthur Brown, Jr., architect of City Hall, and Henry Howard, the son of John Galen Howard, supervising architect of the University of California at Berkeley. In Gold Rush days, flags were flown from atop Telegraph Hill to notify the city that a ship from the States was entering the Golden Gate. As the signature feature atop Telegraph Hill on the northeastern skyline, Coit Tower proudly proclaims San Francisco to vessels passing to and from the ports of the East Bay. Between today's Coit Tower and the Gold Rush flagpole there exists a functional continuity. The work of signaling exits and entrances continues.

The Marriott Hotel, a neo–Art Deco jukebox of a building, represents the most recent and most exuberant addition to the postmodern San Francisco skyline. Hotels have always played a major role in the city's identity and economy, beginning with such Victorian hostelries as the Lick House, the Baldwin House, the What Cheer House, and the Palace Hotel. The elegant Fairmont atop Nob Hill, a masterpiece of *belle époque* luxury, fortunately survived the 1906 earthquake, although the ensuing fire gutted its unfinished interior. Tourism is evident as well in the logo of Fisherman's Wharf, where millions of visitors are welcomed each year, and by the symmetrically stacked piles of crabs and T-shirts awaiting tourist attention.

Temperate weather makes San Francisco a wonderful city in which to walk or otherwise traverse the streets. So many modern cities have lost their "walkability" in wholesale surrender to the automobile, but not San Francisco. In the 1960s, in fact, the city stopped a freeway that was supposed to run through town to the Golden Gate Bridge. The city abounds in pedestrian-oriented public places, most of them graced by fountains and statuary. An original casting of Rodin's *The Thinker* graces the entrance of the California Palace of the Legion of Honor. A statue of Christopher Columbus gazes out to sea from the base of Coit Tower. In Union Square, the Greek goddess of victory, a trident in one hand and a laurel wreath in the other, celebrates the victory of Commodore George Dewey at Manila Bay. On Market Street muscled and sinewy mechanics work at an industrial press, in a monument by Douglas Tilden, one of San Francisco's most noted fin de siècle artists. In Ghirardelli Square, a delightful mermaid cavorts with sea turtles in the midst of a circular fountain by Ruth Asawa.

In addition to statues and fountains, other pleasures awaiting the pedestrian in San Francisco are its trees, parks, and gardens. Monterey cypress trees assume Dante-esque shapes along the esplanade encircling Sutro Heights. A stand of Monterey pine fronts a boulevard lined with multicolored neo-Mediterranean bungalows of the sort that dominate the residential districts west of Twin Peaks. Douglas fir, pine, and eucalyptus trees enrich residential hilltops. A solitary fan palm stands sentry along the Filbert Steps. At Portsmouth Square in Chinatown, pruned sycamores await the sproutings of spring against a background dominated by the tallest building in the city, the headquarters of the San Francisco–founded Bank of America.

Beneath these trees run carpets of flowers and flowering plants, either growing spontaneously or artfully planted. Wildflowers run up the side of Telegraph Hill toward Julius' Castle restaurant and cover the headlands fronting the Golden Gate. Backyards run riot in flowers, ferns, heather, and trees of every description. Each day, Lombard Street attracts hundreds of visitors eager to drive down the zigzag garden that has taken possession of this steep street. Gardens adorn hundreds of courtyards and patios. Flower stands abound downtown.

San Francisco is a city for music, art, and theater—a city that prides itself on its support and enjoyment of the fine and performing arts. On most evenings, Louise M. Davies Symphony Hall will be ablaze in light, as if illuminated by the music itself. Out in the Music Concourse of Golden Gate Park, a space created by the Mid-Winter Exposition of 1894, crowds gather for an afternoon of opera. Across the Concourse a sphinx from that very same Mid-Winter Fair stands guard near the M. H. de Young and Asian Art museums. Based on the Avery Brundage Collection, the Asian is the finest single comprehensive collection of Asian art in the world. With the gift of the Mr. and Mrs. John D. Rockefeller III Collection of American Art in the late 1970s, the de Young began a journey toward its present status as one of the most noted American art museums in the country.

San Francisco is graced by some of the most beautiful synagogues in the nation, including Sherith Israel on California Street and Emanu-El at Lake and Arguello, two congregations founded during the Gold Rush. Glistening in the sunlight, onion-shaped spires surmounted by Orthodox crosses suggest the strong Russian presence in the city, dating from an influx of immigrants after the Russian Revolution of 1917 and the ensuing civil war. The Arabian Nights exoticism of the Vedanta Society's old headquarters on Filbert Street testifies to the city's established receptivity to eastern thought. Saint Mary's Cathedral, by contrast, anticipates in its bold futurity a Christianity as concerned with the future as with the past. Here is a cathedral inspired by Teilhard de Chardin: a sacred place seeking to illuminate, not only a historic creed but also the natural origins of religion in our sense of awe before the cosmos—its stained glass celebrating the elements of earth, air, fire, and water. Of all major cathedrals in America, St. Mary's is the most architecturally courageous and hence it speaks in some degree to that optimism before the future which abides in the San Francisco psyche with an equally powerful tendency to conserve that which already is. From this perspective, San Francisco is a self-conscious city, a connoisseur of its own beauty and reputation.

There also flourishes a San Francisco of multi-ethnic striving, of new Americans emerging enthusiastically into their unfolding identity. Demographics suggest that this impending San Francisco will be predominantly Asian in population and ambiance. The aesthetics of this perception begin in the Japanese Tea Garden in Golden Gate Park, yet another legacy of the Mid-Winter Exhibition. The Hagiwara family tended this garden on a volunteer basis for three generations, as if to keep cultivated the aesthetic legacy of Japan in America at a time of impeded dialogue. Chinese San Francisco flourished more openly, and Santi Visalli has captured its balance of restraint and exotic luxuriance.

American flags flying atop a house on California Street and a Nob Hill hotel and from the stern of a bay vessel support the Americanness of San Francisco amidst its ethnic diversity. This is a city, after all, that was acquired at the height of Manifest Destiny, when the United States envisioned itself as a continental nation fronting the Pacific. One hundred and fifty years later, ironies abound. The Mexico from which California and San Francisco were seized now partially reclaims its lost possession through the presence of a vigorous Hispanic community. A city which persecuted its Chinese residents in the 1870s and played a leading role in banishing Chinese immigration altogether in the 1880s today sustains a vibrant Chinese population and is a favorite arena of investment for Hong Kong and Taiwan.

The complexities and paradoxes of San Francisco reflect the larger polycultural drama of the nation, which first raised its Stars and Stripes in Portsmouth Square on 9 July 1846. Whatever else it is, San Francisco is an American city—a little more exotic than its inland counterparts and certainly a little more beautiful. This unique gift of beauty and cultural complexity does not detach San Francisco from the larger American experiment. San Francisco is a world city in an American context. It sits squarely in the symbolic center of one of the major metropolitan regions of the nation. Day by day, it carries on the ordinary work of American cities. The gift of beauty can sometimes render San Francisco a little too self-regarding, but this same gift of beauty can also energize the collective civic life of San Francisco with a special sense of purpose. The world expects much of San Francisco. So much, after all, has been given to this city in the way of beauty and civic style. Welcoming millions of visitors each year is San Francisco's way of saying thanks.

Pages 14–15. Skyline views from the Hilton Hotel's Cityscape Restaurant

Pages 20–21. A row of restored Victorian houses facing Alamo Square

Pages 22–23. Fog rolls in over the Marin headlands and the Golden Gate Bridge

Page 25. City Hall (1915), by Bakewell and Brown, modeled after the U.S. Capitol Building

Pages 26–27. The Palace of Fine Arts (1915), by Bernard Maybeck, built for the Panama-Pacific International Exposition of 1915

Pages 28–29. San Francisco Bay seen from Pacific Heights

Page 30. Golden Gate Theatre (1922), detail
Page 31. Mission High School (1926), detail

Page 38. The Ritz-Carlton San Francisco Hotel (1909), originally home to the Metropolitan Life insurance company

Page 39 (top). Bank of California (1908), detail, by Bliss and Faville

Page 39 (bottom). Shell Building (1929), detail, by George Kelham

Pages 40–41. Edmund G. Brown State Office Building (1986), by Skidmore, Owings & Merrill

Page 42. *The Mechanic's Monument* (1895), by Douglas Tilden, on Market Street

Page 43. Pagoda, Chinatown

Pages 52, 53. A yellow cab hurtles down California Street on Nob Hill, past a Gothic Revival apartment building. Moments later, a cable car heads uphill at a slower pace.

Page 60. The entrance to Chinatown is marked by ornate lanterns

Page 61. A monastery sits atop a bank in Chinatown

Page 62. The Cannery, near Fisherman's Wharf, built in 1909, houses shops, art galleries, and unique restaurants

Page 63. Mermaids cavort with sea turtles in Ruth Asawa's sculpture at Ghirardelli Square

Pages 64–65. A flower display at the Conservatory in Golden Gate Park honors the San Francisco 49ers

A sphinx outside the M. H. de Young Memorial Museum in Golden Gate Park

Pages 68–69. *El Cid,* in Lincoln Park, commands a panoramic view of the Golden Gate

Page 71. Sailing on San Francisco Bay

The Sentinel Building and the Transamerica Pyramid (1972), by William Pereira and Associates

The Transamerica Pyramid seen from Chinatown

Page 74. One of the new generation of Financial District skyscrapers

Page 75. The Marriott Hotel on Market Street (1989) has been described as a giant jukebox

Pages 76–77. The financial district skyline, with Coit Tower and Alcatraz Island in the distance

Page 78. An aerial view of Lombard Street

Page 79. The famous "zigzag garden" of Lombard Street

Page 81. The grand rotunda entrance to the Neiman Marcus department store at Union Square

Page 82. The end of a school day at Everett Middle School

Page 83. The Palace of Fine Arts

Page 84. Intermission at the War Memorial Opera House

Page 85. Detail of the ornate lobby ceiling at the former head-quarters of Pacific Bell, 140 New Montgomery Street

Pages 86–87. Telegraph Hill at sunrise

Page 93. The Union Oil tower at the approach to the San Francisco–Oakland Bay Bridge

Page 94. The Geary Theater, longtime home of the renowned American Conservatory Theater, was damaged in the 1989 earthquake

Page 95. Entrance to the Fairmont Hotel at the top of Nob Hill

Pages 98, 99. Victorians line the streets near Alamo Square

Pages 100–101. Molinari's, a well-stocked North Beach grocery and deli

Page 102. Japanese Tea Garden, Golden Gate Park

Page 103. Flower Garden at the entrance of the Golden Gate Bridge

Page 105. The downtown office and courtyard of lawyer Melvin Belli

Page 106. Third Church of Christ Scientist on Haight Street

Page 107. An ornate stained-glass window, a typical Victorian detail

Page 108. Golden Gate Theatre, detail

Page 109. The Flood Building, at Hallidie Plaza on Market Street

Pages 110–11. The stars and stripes and Alcatraz Island

Pages 112–13. The Vedanta Society Old Temple at Filbert and Webster streets

Page 120. The U.S. Coast Guard patrolling the bay

Page 121. Commuters with their morning coffee on the ferry from Sausalito

Pages 122–23. Grant Street, Chinatown's crowded main thoroughfare

Page 124. Sunday brunch at Lehr's Greenhouse Restaurant in the Canterbury Hotel on Sutter Street

Page 125. Brother Paul Bernardino of the Franciscan Brothers and Sisters

Page 127. Tennis and spectacular views at Buena Vista Park

Pages 128–29. Sutro Heights Park on a Sunday afternoon

Pages 130–31. Stanford University, in nearby Palo Alto, boasts intricately detailed Spanish Revival architecture

Pages 132, 133. The Conservatory in Golden Gate Park,
modeled after the Palm House in London's Kew Gardens

Pages 150–51. Dixieland jazz at the Gold Dust Lounge on Powell Street

Page 153. Pipe organ inside the modern St. Mary's Cathedral (1971)

Page 154. Louise M. Davies Symphony Hall (1980), by Skidmore, Owings & Merrill

Page 155. The Ferry Building (1894), by Arthur Page Brown, modeled after the campanile of the Cathedral of Seville

Windy evening at the Top of the Mark, the skyline bar atop the Mark Hopkins Hotel

Pages 164–65. The San Francisco–Oakland Bay Bridge at sunset

Page 167. The Shaklee Building, Market Street

Pages 168–69. New skyscrapers in the Financial District

A pruned sycamore in front of the Bank of American Building (1969)

Roof garden at the Crocker Galleria

Page 172. The Russ Building (1928), by George Kelham
Page 173. Streetlights by Bliss and Faville on Union Square

Entry lamps at 115 Sansome Street

Page 194. A panoramic view of Marin County from atop the south tower of the Golden Gate Bridge

Page 195. Oversize cables suspend the Golden Gate Bridge's roadway

Pages 196, 197. Details and views of the Golden Gate Bridge

Pages 198–99. The Golden Gate Bridge at sunset

Pages 200, 201. Views of the Golden Gate Bridge

Pages 202–7. The Golden Gate Bridge at sunset, sunrise, and midday

ACKNOWLEDGMENTS

Since my first visit to San Francisco, during my honeymoon thirty years ago, I have been in love with this city. It reminds me of certain coastal towns in Sicily, where I grew up. Although its topography, architecture, and people are different, other things, such as the smell of saline water, the cable car bells (so much like those of the old Italian trams), and many of the moods and the feelings they elicit are the same. San Francisco seems to me an American invention of a Mediterranean city, and I always feel at home here.

It was with great anticipation that I set about to do this book, which took almost two years. I hope I have done justice to the Pearl of the Pacific. But all I accomplished would never have been possible without the generous help of many San Franciscans and a few very dear friends.

Special thanks go to Jane and Dan Pavone for showing me some lovely spots. Thanks go also to Sean and Basia Randolph for keeping me posted on special events, accompanying me on weekend excursions—even in the chilliest, dense fog—and providing warm friendship. Thank you to the Fairmont and Hilton Hotels for making my stays comfortable. Thank you to Ms. Robin Eickman, Motion Picture Coordinator of the Office of the Mayor. Thank you to Mr. Robert Warren, Manager of the Golden Gate Bridge, for allowing me to climb the 740 feet of the bridge's south tower. And thank you to Kevin Starr for his introduction to this book.

I would also like to thank all the people who appear in this book and the owners of numerous buildings who gave me special permission for photographing. An affectionate thank you goes to my son, Ivon, who drove up from Los Angeles several times to assist me and who took the portrait for the jacket of this book. Thank you to my publisher, Charles Miers; my editors, Jen Bilik and Jim Stave; the designer Gilda Hannah; and the rest of the staff at Universe.

Santi Visalli